# Praise

"This is a collection that sustains itself admirably, not an inch of give in its tautly turned lines, not a scintilla of precision out of place. More than consummate craft, I think this tendency displays a rare patience and generosity of attention; the respect that poetry owes to the world. Here is a world we recognise, but few have the guts or the skill to set it down like this: so fresh, so frightening, so hauntingly familiar."

Fran Lock

"These poems balance deftly between transience and appetite, between the clarity of distance and the energy of immediate sensations. Whether the material is from memory or other lives like Chaplin's or Bowie's glimpsed through the curtains of their fame, whether the setting is the local pub or a thousand miles away, the gaze is unassuming and acute, inviting those sparks of connection when the subject looks back from the page with a life of its own."

Philip Gross

"Alan Humm's poems come from a place of affinity with life's outsiders: the drunkards, the dreamers, the brilliant, the flawed—the jugglers of darkness and light. An intense, intelligent and intoxicating new collection from a poet who knows the ropes."

Maggie Sawkins

# About the Author

Alan Humm edits the arts journal *One Hand Clapping*. *My Father is Calling the Neighbours Names* is his second collection of poetry, the first being *A Brief and Biased History of Love* (Published by Culture Matters). *The Sparkler*, his first novel, was published by Vine Leaves Press in 2024 and his second novel, *Rough Music*, is due to be published in 2026.

*alanhummswriting.com*

# *My* Father *is* Calling *the* Neighbours Names

Alan Humm

**My Father is Calling the Neighbours Names**

Print Edition
ISBN: 978-3-98832-167-1
Published by Vine Leaves Press 2025



Cover design by Jessica Bell
Interior design by Amie McCracken

*“Every limit is a beginning as well as an ending.”*

George Eliot

# Contents

# My Father is Calling the Neighbours Names

Out on the grass
my father is calling the neighbours names,
which is his art.
Softly, he starts to mourn.
The sky's a mild suburban blue,
each lawn so circumspect
it's like a stamp,
but he is being moved
by something subterranean.
Come see: my father is unravelling.
His face is working loose.
Drink has smoothed out his consonants
until his voice is like an oracle,
but in reverse:
a wheel revving through mud,
his curse just so much effluent.
Cruel, to be made to think
that this is speech;
that it is something like a hammer
poised
in his weakly quibbling hand.

# After Larkin

Ever so distant, it isn't me
wallowing in the pull
of summer: gnat-gleam; sunlight taking leaf
in dusty windows and the throbbing light
of piss in open cartons, all arranged
carefully, like cubist washing, in a line.
I used to iron on the floor. I thrived
downstairs. I was all gesture; a parade.
But here, between the boxes, what survived

was almost nothing: hands and teeth and hair.
Nobody came up from the bar or made
so much as a distasteful joke. Beyond the stairs,
I lay entombed. What it all meant
I couldn't say; not there.
But now I hear the drunken moaning of my dad;
I hear their drumbeat in the house next door;
I feel what I refused to feel: how sad I was,
and now I taste the attic's desolate fulfilment.

# Our Old Town

Seen from this distance, the town defers
to… what? Time?
Love? It wavers
like an ember.

The river makes everything riverine:
sunlight wobbling
like a tossed coin;
a slickening shine;

swift sparks — a kind of winnowing.
It's company:
soft hills swell
like something you'd sing.

The bars are lit like nativities;
moonlight is grain
that sifts itself;
the park's a sea

so wide I daren't go back again.
Those misremembered
hills. That light.
Let them remain.

# Ernest

… and in the end you choose
the family you think that you deserve.
It's New Year's Eve. I'm making
lightning in the glass I tilted from the shelf
and caught, one-handed, on the fly.
The bar is cresting, and this man
— the man displaying
a deft crispness at the pump
— is who I think I am.
Ernest unwinds my tie;
whatever boundary I wish to assert,
he's saying, is not welcome here.
Later, he will bestow himself,
his fingers delicately saying yes,
or else he'll sway from side to side:
a wrecking ball.
He'll try to kiss me
and I'll fail to understand.
When I left, he dwindled to thumb
then finger size;
to the size of the man
inside the man pulling the pump.

# In Memoriam

# 1 Pegasus

The bike, the bike's momentum
and the road
are all one thing.
It's like manoeuvres:
every gesture
something that you're swimming in.
You don't heft a gun;
something within you does it.
The *army* does it.
In the kitchen,
you display embarrassment,
your arms so superabundant
that your wife
begins to croon to them.
You make love
with a confidence that's not your own;
wave goodbye
just as though the stolen bike
is Pegasus and you Bellephoron,
which is to say
you fail to be attuned
to the June light;
to the trees

threshing like corn.
The more you are a part
of the machine,
the more you outrun
the world that makes obeisance
in your wake,
the more you feel
the swift pang of mortality
that comes with a daughter
being born.

## 2 D-Day

Babies,
bow-legged
with the weight
of Sten guns,
Bren guns,
hand grenades and magazines.
There is no moon:
each face,
covered in cork,
is like a patch of darkness
broken off.
There's air
here in your chest,
so that, when you piss,
it feels like it's just that,
its scuttering line,
that tethers you
to the ground.
In the glider, Players
cigarettes and the daft
syncopation of "Cow Cow Boogie".
If you can hear your voice
then you're still here.

You've never experienced
another's arm as being so warm.

No flak: an open corridor,
the glider bumping
blindly against the backrush
of the plane. Again and then again
then silence.
You are easing down,
a lover, into the lower air.

Where were you?
Were you the boy
who feigned a limp?
The one who lay
inside a shellhole
clutching his hands
in prayer? Or did you
breast the air
as though it had
the cleanness of a wave?
Did you see the tank,
its brocade of colour,
as it exploded?
No, I see no difference:
if you had cowered,
we could have joked
about it later on.
You were gunned down,
anyway, at Escoville.
I have a picture of your face,
its wry, hopeful regard,

and wonder how it felt
to be squeezed through
that giant door:
the infinite black sky
without the usual troop of stars.

# Margalef

I lay at three o'clock as though the beer
had tripped me up. Drinking was irresistible:
an answer to the softness of the call
of evening light, the way it salves the sheer
sides of the sky; the aching trees and leaves,
soft silt, no longer blaring in the sun.
The long day too. The way it had begun
in cliffs and scrub; the saddening purple sheen
of mountains stacked, like washing, in the air
and our rock face: the holes that looked like holds
but were all rock. Glib, almost: hole after hole.
Aloof as only nature is. Outstaring
us. We eked each move along the face,
securing every step; knowing our place.

# Hemingway

His body is a verb,
beard blossoming like a taunt,
delirious on his face.

Such frail construction:
how a fish, as iridescent as a rainbow,
and a blunt cigar, a genuflecting bull,
are all supposed to mean the things you are;
how just one adjective,
like dye in water,
can alter everything.

# To My Daughter on Her Eighteenth Birthday

Outside, the noise of cars;
stars shaken out of reach;
footsteps naming a kind of peace:
inhabited space.
Sometimes I wonder
if it lurks in me, the lack
my flat's supposed to represent:
the sudden shock of the TV,
the blur of old appliances,
the only sound;
my books' bright spines
staving off vacancy.

But, see, I'm not alone.
Love comes, and when it goes
it lingers in the camber
of the furniture;
in me; in memory.
Meanwhile, your elsewhere's
always in my head.
You are my ballast,

as I am yours,
and, yes, the phone's
sometimes a barrier,
each pause a weight
I've had to learn to lift,
but I don't think it matters
all that much.

I love you;
it's simple enough.
Wherever you go,
no loneliness so deep
you can't row back to me.
Imagine the glow,
still there,
of the remembered sun;
the lights,
their bright
and undiminished heat,
beside the motorway:
no matter how diffuse
and far away they seem,
they're always there,
casting their light against the dark.
They'll always
always
guide you home.

# Charlie

## 1

His mother
acted out the crucifixion:
Christ's face
with the pallor
of an East End waif.
He was in need of bloaters;
ham and eggs.
Legs pressed together,
arms outstretched,
she vexed herself to bursting;
sang without using her voice.
Cloistered behind curtains,
she'd act out the street.
She could be anything —
sunlight; a copper's nark —
and afterwards,
playing in the park,
Charlie looked at her hands,
the way they fluttered
as she fed the pigeons
then refused to settle down.
He saw how she became herself
when she was least herself.

No words:
simply the briefest rainbow
arched above
the pitiful patter of the birds.

## 2

Once, in the park,
his brother made a ball
of newspaper and string.
One thing become another,
just as though,
glazed by the sun,
it advertised another life.
Banks; restaurants;
an affluent woman's face
forced you to feel invisible.
Nothing was what it was:
it grew or shrank
in the uneven light
of your regard.
If you were poor,
your longing burnished every crumb.
You lost yourself
trying to bridge the gap.
Later, he danced with everything,
his talent —
an assiduous burnishing —
no different from love.

## 3

His mother faltered.
Now the audience was as unstable
as the sea.
He couldn't wait:
paraded; thumbed his waistcoat;
sang "'e don't know 'oo 'e is."
His frame aspired upwards
while his hands polished his coat.
He waded in a flood of money;
sang and sang again,
each song a prayer
for what continued to be thrown,
as tangible as grace,
from the insouciant gods.

## 4

At eight,
he danced in clogs,
one cog in a machine,
bright as a flame
lost in a fire.
Soon he would learn to mould the air
around him into an orchestra;
to carve a loaf of bread
into a concertina's folds.
He was as tense
and as responsive
as a tuning fork.
He only had to walk
to hear the pits roar.
Reams of white paper,
ragged light,
confettied him,
each of his gestures
as inflated and precise
as when a groom
accepts a wedding ring;
smooths it
for one slow inch
along a finger's seam.

## 5

America!
Department stores so full
it was like being smothered
in a dream.
The thickness of the shirts;
the light tread
of the shopwalkers,
like doctors
yielding to their patients' call.
Outside, the buildings
all burlesqued him;
pushed against the sky
as though urging to be let in.
The cars; the cops;
the night ablaze
with being,
every lightbulb flooded
with its need to shine,
he lived there
like a bird
lives on a branch.
He didn't trust it;
loved it, partly,

because he didn't;
because he knew
it would be snatched away.
Each door,
each brightly burnished gate,
as tempting as a coin
and just as likely to depreciate.

## 6

Stanley Jefferson
lies in his bed
and counts his toes.
He's watching Charlie
gloss his face
with cork. He knows
how every gesture is a fluent phrase,
speaking the truth
of someone else's face.
But there is something else:
a fire. A brazen dare. A need.
Charlie's features come to life
in the same way that movie light
ignites a strip of celluloid.
He turns his head
and there are glimmers of this;
glimmers of that.
Even his hat's alive.
He is starlight to Stanley's donkey.
Now they're due on stage.
Hurriedly, Stan dons his apparel.
It will be years
before he is Stan Laurel.

## 7

In Hollywood,
each set
is open to the elements.
The wind plays
with an actor's hair;
it lifts the tablecloth
and fusses with the rug.
Sometimes the unit
jumps into a truck
and drives to where
stark scrubland frames a space
as blank as any stage.
Charlie can front the wind
and bump against it like a kite.
The light —
that broad unyielding loud
American light —
seems given to him
to juggle or display.
He forces himself on film,
slows it to suit the pace
his shoes dictate.
Those splayed and outsize shoes,

like balancing on fish.
Watch how the racetrack crowd
begin to understand
that everything revolves
around the little guy:
the horses and the endless sky,
the camera, all in thrall
to Charlie,
who, they will soon realise,
is all of life
and all its hardships
rolled
into one bouncing ball.

## 8

Old film is like a grave
in which the dead still move.
Difficult to believe in love
when boy and girl
are only wraiths,
and, anyway, styles change.
You have to trust
that Edna isn't meant
to be this matronly.
It is, that beauty now,
more in the way Charlie reacts
than in her face.
He swoons while standing up.
She flares then sways and yields
as though she is precisely
what he feels;
smiles like she is expressing
his own heat.
Later, she drank.
Her beauty, so much filigree,
became illegible.
Look, though, and you can read
her mouth's dismay;

the way her eyes still hope.
She hasn't died.
She rises
from the ashes
of forgotten days,
as frail as smoke.

## 9

Marriage a lightness,
like a coat worn carelessly,
and then one note —
Charlie; Charlie; Charlie —
sounding in the poor girl's ear.
Each girl lost
in the fierceness of his need
to be himself;
to be so free
he was exemplary
while being treated like a king.
Each bed a trap.
Each wedding ring
a snake
that he was scared
would take him by the throat.
Each new life
like a bit of business
he would briefly own
and then discard.
Mildred, Lita, Paulette:
so many orts and scraps.

## 10

A paradox: the silliness of rolls
made into dainty feet
but rendered with such purity
that all you hear's the music
that the hands create.
It's a new kind of elegance,
born out of poverty;
out of the things
that you can only see
with the mind's flickering light.
He walks
just like he's striking music
from the world's behind,
his hands prosaic miracles:
proof that we are the only miracle
we need;
that we can make new worlds,
bright skeins of smoke,
out of the fragile promise of the air.

## 11

Outside,
the orange groves mark time.
Inside, Charlie proceeds to count it;
is so proud of his own studio
he films it going up,
the opposite
of something flowering;
its walls definitively closed.
It's home, transposed,
time ticking to his will:
everything in motion
and then stilled,
kept static,
'til he sets it going
like a clock.
Each whim is set in stone.
Nevertheless, the fluent groves
outlasted him.

## 12

Cocteau
met Chaplin. Said:
"I don't speak English.
He doesn't speak French.
We talked
without the slightest difficulty.
Words caught the light.
He would transport them
from one language to another.
Sometimes, a gesture
would precede a word;
it would escort it.
There was no slowness,
only the apparent slowness
of the balls
when a juggler
disciplines them,
one slow ball after another,
in the air."

## 13

*Limelight.*
Both men so singular
you'd hardly call it
a duet.
More and more difficult at Charlie's age
to place yourself, foursquare,
upon a stage
and mimic flight.
Keaton looks blind;
it is the world we laugh at,
how it conspires
to trap him, like a bird.
Charlie's hands
barely belong to him;
he eyes them with as much distrust
as if his fingers
are a pair of snapping jaws.
Pause, and you see
how everything is loss.
His cheeks proclaim it,
and his eyes.
He falls into the pit
and we are anxious that he is alright,

this old man
conjuring his youth
with such ferocity
we see how age
drags on him like a stone.

## 14

If Charlie's pathos
seems unearned, consider this:
in every building,
tall and grandiose,
he saw its opposite:
the dust
that floated in its wake.
Some places push their chests out;
seem to speak.
Others are dumb.
Charlie gave voice to those,
and so America abandoned him.
In Switzerland, in his last week,
he lay and dozed
and listened to how voices
can conceal a room;
felt, for one last time,
how all the things you know
only reveal themselves
on the vast loom of silence.

# The Drummer on the Bridge

For Naomi

The drummer on the bridge
begins a roll
that sounds like "yes"
but is so slurry
that his loneliness is everywhere.

I love him
for the time it takes
to get to the other side.
You are nearby.
You come into my arms
as easily as if you are
a thought being condensed
here in my hands.

Me? I am built on sand
but, caught within the logic
of each other's arms,
you make the thing I am

seem like a drum roll;
like the bubble of air
that divers keep
inside their mouths
for safety
on their long ascent
towards the sky.

## Chessington

The otter hits the water,
wears it like a skin,
then makes the bank
and leaps,
cracking its body like a whip.

Elsewhere, there's a recording
of a lion's roar,
a signature
so densely present that the lion
seems discarded; someone else's toy.

Everywhere, the opposite of experience.
Music, its tangled wool
supposed to fool you into thinking
you're in Singapore.
The blurriness of water

wagging through a tiger's mouth
isn't the same.
Ferocious but still tame,
it is as much like the otter
as a recumbent flag.

# Kyoto

It was my first earthquake. The building seemed
to slip then right itself. It made me feel
like I'd been thrown and caught. But that was Kyoto:
everything balancing. The temple was doubled
on the lake, stones floated in sand
and the rake's contrails drew the eye to rest
in something like infinity. In the river, a heron
rested on another heron, done
in oil, while our guide teetered precariously;
professed to be a connoisseur but really
was addicted to the way a geisha's
neck can seem to float above her dress;
the way her hand, when moving, seems to fly:
to flow and rest, a bird trapped in the sky.

# Phuket

His feet fondle the sand but then
his toes express distaste. Sea wrack
and a slick, quickening line and
then the sea itself, collapsing and
collapsing. Even at Pi-pi,
each fish a fanfare,
he's afraid he will allow
himself to be dragged down.

The tarmac shimmers like a looking
glass. Step through it and the bars,
like giant sideboards, line the streets.
Some girls are really boys, their arms and
legs as sleek as if they had been dragged
through fire or water. He is taller; thinner.
He must be: voices bubble in his wake.

Each bar enacts itself. Old men,
stubby as thumbs, drag girls from
side to side. Shake a girl here
and she'll pretend to fizz.
He tuts, and rolls his eyes,
but in the end what he feels
is something like aspiration.

He climbs a flight of stairs;
enters a room which seems
to be an aspect of himself.
Desire breathes for him;
it speaks for him.
The girl nibbles his lower lip
and there's a moment
(a roiling boil) when he expects
something miraculous:
a transformation.
Soon, all he wants is skin
— just that: skin — but, afterwards,
he doesn't know what to do with her.
He smiles, and pats something.
On her arm, he has left a slick,
quickening line.

## Woolwich

The river, like stroked fur,
is silver in the places
where the wind has touched it.
Tate & Lyle;
Canary Wharf;
the Barrier — all are diminished
by the river's breadth.
The world is larger
than you think. The sky
is its own echo, endlessly
reiterating nothing and imposing nothing.
Here, hunched up against the wall,
a rustbucket, the Royal Iris,
tilted in the foreground. Rust a curse:
time's judgement, or time's echo,
parodying towers
that look like brushstrokes,
asserting nothing.

# The Grand Canyon

It was just after 9/11. Drawings of eagles
hovered everywhere. "This," our pilot
said, "is how Santa Claus flies over Afghanistan."
EE-stan, like a cowboy song. We surfed the scrub.
Earlier we had ascended to the sound
of horns; it was as though we, and not the canyon,
were the miracle: as though we were as inevitable
as the sun rising. Vegas in the day was just a landing
pad. Chastened by light, it didn't know
what it was supposed to be. But at night it had
the tarnished glamour of hocked jewellery.
The American Way: either this, its promiscuous glitter,
or the Hoover Dam; the brightness of its austerity.
An archangel gathering its wings? Or plain old destiny?

# Elvis

My dad is keening;
snuffling into the light.
His voice is resonating
in his headphones
like it would in church.

What we hear, though, is a groan
that gathers momentum
and then crashes;
splutters like a failing tyre.
It's odd: the music is so bland.
The bass does baby steps.
Each tune is like an illustration
of a tune. Elvis, but Elvis in Bacofoil;
*opera buffa* Elvis.

Beer confers greatness.
The radiogram; his bucket chair:
these are his kingdom. The lamp
leans over him, but his voice
won't do his bidding.
Soon he will weep.
Insufficient unto the day
is the lack of expression thereof.

# Thirteen Ways of Looking at David Bowie

## 1 Top of the Pops

**S**ly lights pick out
**T**ensions between the raw and cooked.
**A**ssonance: the same old gestures but
**R**efined; containing
**M**ore: something that's flaunted like a dare.
**A**udience members all stare solemnly.
**N**oli me tangere. But soon: acceptance, meaning renewal.

# 2 Julie*

His silence was so loud.
It was a question of glazing over
and becoming incoherent.
People had to prod me.
I used to think he was the Coming of the Lord.
We'd have this wonderful space age relationship.

I tried to masturbate.
I thought: if it's truly possible to walk through glass
and reach him
I might touch him.
For a long time I used a hairbrush.
I used to think about a cold, hard atmosphere
with a lot of cloud.
I had orgasms of a space kind;
non-committed hysteria.
I would lie under the covers for fear
of being overwhelmed.

He was there for me.

I was humming.
I'd think this means this and this means that.

I'd think of ESP.
I had conversations with him.
I used to walk around the room
protecting my small parts.
He'd say, "Well, I have to leave you now."

I was crying a lot,
we were all crying,
because of Ziggy.
He'd tease people
by holding out his hand to them.
I remember going home as all fans do,
in solitary confinement.

He prompted something in me.

I never believed I was David Bowie.

It's a terrible thing he did really.

He has a lot to answer for.

**A redaction of "Julie: He's Got a Lot to Answer For" from* Starlust: The Secret Fantasies of Fans *by Fred and Judy Vermorel. You can find the extract in* The Faber History of Pop, *edited by Hanif Kureishi and Jon Savage and published by Faber & Faber in 1995.*

# 3 Bowie and Me

My girlfriend bought me *Aladdin Sane*.
It was meant, I think,
to be exemplary: what could be sexier?
Not sex, which vexed us both.
The songs wallowed in something
that was like another atmosphere.
It wasn't, quite, desire;
more like heat:
the opposite of us.
The music mussed the room
just as, you felt, Bowie could smear
himself — that musk
the famous have,
as pungent as the smell
of roasting meat —
just about everywhere.
My romance didn't last,
but Bowie did.
The things that were hidden from me then
are what I love about him now:
the way his songs
disclose a taut inscrutability;
hang there like oil in water; overlap;

explore terrains you've never thought about before.
*Aladdin Sane*? It's still cocksure.
But there is something else.
Unease. Distrust.
The transience you meet
trying to find yourself
in the mirror's maze.
(Whose face? It never lets you see.)
All of the things I felt
coming to terms with what I didn't know,
there on my girlfriend's bed.

# 4 Singer on National Network Experiences Trauma

I mime delirium, distaste, and then
stare at the host; my underwater stare.
I'm floating here, the real is over there;
nothing but real; a feint; a holding pen.
I place a finger on my brow; attempt a smile.
I feel how tight the skin is on my face,
and how the tall lamps blast my panstick beige
wet forehead white as a bland bathroom tile.
Later, after the make-up girl has gone,
trapped in my living room, I try to feel
the stars gutter and brim; try to explain
how every iridescent self is one
attempt to mine, or to locate, the real
here in my floundering, unyielding brain.

## 5 Blackstar

Yes, something happened on the day he died.
Something was let out of the world, like air
from a balloon. We cried, mostly, for us:
for all those times the world was just an echo,
dully reverberant, and he'd proclaim
himself our avatar; would ease the passage
from our world to his: the rain no longer
just the dull gloss on the known, but stage rain;
something like an accompaniment. He *unfurled* himself.
Sometimes, he lost a step, but at the last
he leapt again into the inhospitable:
music like the slow unyielding music
of a storm. On the day he died, he was ours
again, just like he always knew he would be.

## 6 Live Aid

Something like calm; something like peace
adheres; disdaining artifice

he seems to greet us face to face.
Consoling, legible, he makes

a perfect silhouette: foursquare
and elegant; emphatically here.

But this is artificial too:
his hair like gold, his teeth like new,

the way he smiles, as though each song
is logical as stepping stones.

Too sly and fey to make us think
of Everyman, he's Bowie Inc.

# 7 Insomniacs

## With apologies to A. E. Stallings

Lover, I will not linger.
I turn my moon-cold shoulder.
Why would you trust a singer?
The room is getting colder.

I turn my moon-cold shoulder.
I make free with the cover.
The room is getting colder.
Go find another lover.

I make free with the cover.
There are so many of you.
Go find another lover.
I cannot hope to love you.

There are so many of you.
So many lonely places.
Go find another lover;
Find sympathetic faces.

So many lonely places.
Lover, I will not linger.
Find sympathetic faces.
Why would you trust a singer?

# 8 Terry

It's difficult to explain
how the world cracks open,
disclosing fire.
A band, that's all,
their noise, explicable —
loud bass and drums;
lightning on the guitar —
became unbearable.
Thunder, inside,
there in his brother's brain.
The sly, tilting kiss of madness.
Bowie ran; was always running:
bright star; blind mole.
Each act,
each iridescent character,
formed in the void;
the lone self's howling wind.

The lone self's howling wind
formed in the void.
Each iridescent character,
each act:
bright star; blind mole.

Bowie ran from it; was always running;
the sly tilting kiss of madness
there in his brother's brain.
Thunder, inside,
became unbearable.
Lightning on the guitar;
loud bass and drums;
their noise explicable —
a band, that's all,
disclosing fire.
How the world cracks open.
It's difficult to explain.

# 9 Salute

All hail our visiting Superman,
there in the haven of his car.
He drove out of Victoria
erased and burnished by the sun.
He stood and smiled and waved; no more.
The papers called it a salute.

They made it look like a salute;
like something done by Superman:
his hand and posture somehow more
than someone waving in his car.
He looked like he'd stepped from the sun
to gather us in Victoria,

to *rally* us in Victoria;
to throw the kind of wild salute
associating you with sun
and moon and stars; with Superman.
He was as burnished as his car,
and we were all expecting more.

More what? I couldn't say. Just more.
More than a man in Victoria.

He was as burnished as his car.
He waved. It felt like a wild salute.
And, anyway, we expected Superman.
He shone, for us, just like the sun.

His urge was somehow to be sun
and moon and stars. But claim that more's
been given you, that you're a Superman,
and you end up with Victoria:
with people seeing a wild salute
when you're just waving from your car.

Look at it from our side. Your car,
erased and burnished by the sun,
seemed in itself a wild salute.
Reading the newspapers, what more
could we have asked from Victoria
than that you claimed us like a Superman?

You said it: Homo Superior. Superman
is as Superman does. Less is more
when you wave from a car here in Victoria.

## 10 Home

See him, if you can, at home but not at home, in the 1960s. How much like prose it was, all of those rooms, acoustics like labouring machinery, in which he played the blues. Or oozed over the stage, miming… I don't know what. The Fall of Stalingrad. The Pentateuch. Forget the strange poetry of the later years; the way that he stood, as sinuous and distant as a flame, catching the air between his teeth. No. Try to imagine Davey Jones still poking through. Just like the rest of us: those for whom home felt like a closing jaw; from whom the slightest thing — an armchair or a lighter, say, displayed to signify the family — withdrew. From which we then withdrew in turn. With drugs, was it, for you? A brand new suit? For me, it was the songs. No, not the words: the tunes. As sinuous and distant as a flame, but always there. Always, forever, true. Foursquare. Bowie was home.

## 11 Bar Fly

He was a slab, this guy. Pure prose. Red in the face with the effort
of being him. We need an erotics of David Bowie: how he enters
the blood, like wine. Just for a moment, he was giddy; slightly
out of true. A slab, yes, but there was something around the
eyes, and at his jaw. He was in a band. Was more, he
was implying; much much more. Slowly, he kissed
his beer. He started to describe his friend, the
one who had worked with Bowie. His
hands, two slabs, dipped briefly,
elegantly, towards the bar.
They were mimicking
DB; his talent:
how free it
was. The
fruit
mac
hine
succ
umb
ed to
song.
And I
saw, in the pewter
afternoon, what I should
have seen all along: reflected light.

# 12 Hermeneutics

The soul, on its way
through, craves stasis; craves movement.
Sings its dilemma.

# 13 Beautiful

"He's beautiful," my lover says.
I say: "A mess.

Look, darling. Look at his fingernails."
"Shh. He's ideal."

He's *an* ideal, she means: an imprimatur.
I imagine a cat-purr

Of satisfaction as he sees the cloth
Of his soft

dimpled suit fossick and dip
on his cantered hip.

Square-jawed and somehow feminine,
unfair how in-

candescent he can appear. Those eyes.
And each surprise,

each shimmering suit of clothes, each whim,
became him.

He drew them into him somehow.
I tell her how

he seems to have slept his way to fame.
It's what he became,

that shimmering thing, that she can see.
So unlike me.

# Mrs McDonald

Was that her name?
She was cottony; kittenish.
We used to huddle around her voice
for warmth.
Outside, suburban trees urbanely
gestured in the rain
but, in here, Mrs McDonald's voice
was everything.
Steam clogged the windows.
"... and the king," she said, "could close his eyes
and wish his kingdom anywhere."
He was a nervous king:
his castle bounced from place to place,
and so did we —
we were soldiers; courtiers;
turbulent commoners.
I had a sword; bright epaulettes.
I felt the castle rearing up,
embarrassed (the castle was),
and then I woke
and all the lights were on.
The park had disappeared.
The world was no match

for Mrs McDonald.
I shuffled towards her,
hoping that we'd sing
all of the colours in the windows.

# The Cherry Tree

The pub's become an artefact:
something I lift
to feel the light
pour through the windows.
Every door
led somewhere so coherent
that your posture changed.
In the restaurant
I wore a bright austerity;
a wide non-smile.
The pub like a struck bell,
its slackening air all fag smoke,
felt familial.
More of a tribe than customers,
whatever they were I was.
Flags, I suppose,
waved uselessly.
Baubles were draped
in lightning: tinsel nodding
to those songs
that sound like tills.
Out there, somewhere,
was Christmas; its simplicity.

For me, a cold flat
and a TV as small
as the back of someone's hand.
Warm beer my untranscendent wings,
I sprayed a benediction,
waiting to be inhabited.

# Riley

... runs, then runs,
into the radiant thickness
of the everyday;
tests every moment
in the way she tests
a pile of horse shit
with her tongue. Look at her go,
as though the grass is languishing beneath
the element she's swimming in.
She turns, although it doesn't look like turning;
more a metabolic change — a circuit break.
She watches each breeze stir
like it's about to speak.
When she is poised like this
the world plays on her like a violin.
Look at her eager face.
Look at her lying there,
her paws limp
with the pleasure of surrendering.

# Ferns

New Zealand ferns assent
with thumb and forefinger.
What I remember's tough,
unsentimental names,
water like sprigs of lightning
and glowworms, failing in the dark,
but still the ferns kept saying yes;
kept slowly easing forwards.
They balanced there,
proving how just-about-coherent
nature's incoherence is.

# New York

The Guggenheim unwinds like apple peel
and you assent to what you think it says:
that art, all art, resolves in quietness;
lives out its promise just beside the real.
Meanwhile, New York growls at you like you're food.
It blurts things out: steam; jazz; the noise of trains.
It never pauses for a second. It disdains
stability; hustles towards the sky, no mood
so dense it can't be wished away by height;
by a blithe disregard. Look at Trump's tower,
so ostentatious that it seems austere;
pimped up like someone's car. It just might
be the measure here: art as the opposite of dour
and distant artefacts. Art screaming in your ear.

# American Election (2020)

It felt like something
had bumped the car
but it was just a firework exploding.
You forget how muscular they are:
what you remember is the light.
The car had shrugged;
righted itself;
continued a little more carefully.
Elsewhere, it was still too soon to tell.
You only know
what you've grown used to
when you realise
that you're afraid to hope;
when you attend
to the end of language:
bomb-bursts, and a man receding
in the way that fireworks recede:
corrupted light
and then the residue of light,
its contrails and redundancies,
staining the sky.

# The Colca Canyon

The dark slipped
through the fingers of the moon
like bolts of cloth.
Our guide, Mauricio, had a transistor radio.
The music was astringent and otherworldly.
I wanted to speak to him
but had to console myself with glances;
tender nods.

The colours of the gorge developed:
white to blues and greens.
They began to assert themselves.
So did the drop.
My mule was rolling like a boat at sea.
I gripped its neck.
If I could steer it, I thought,
then I could ride it properly, like a bumper car.

What was its name? George?
Mauricio called it "York."
"Please, York," I said.
"*Please.*"
I was willing it to stay afloat.

I was begging it; crooning, almost.
Its feet were stuttering like castanets.

At the top,
my cheeks are lifted for the camera,
but I am not smiling.
Mauricio and I are separated by
my urge to cry
and his bewilderment.
Later, on the bus, a sign said:
"*Dios es mi co-piloto.*"
He might as well have been.

# Enlightenment

Light quickening the muddy river,
making fishes' scales. The sun's impress
and my stiff sandals, bowling me
from side to side, and the breeze
on the boat: soft hands. Palms;
bougainvillea; buildings like rotting boxes,
and Wat Pho — all efflorescence,
like something blaring outwards.
Dragonish contours, finials like tongues,
and then the golden Buddha, slyly resting
on thin air. Later, I realise that I resent its sculpted smile,
its poise and the assumption that, if you polish
something enough, it will be renewed.
Frayed and unwieldy, I am 52.
My wife and daughter place small coins
in metal boxes. They look like they're planting
something, or attempting to. Unvarnished hope.

# Peru

Stone pressed on stone. No mortar. Friction. Gravity.
And they can move; can use an earthquake as a dancefloor
as they tick, silently, from side to side. Elsewhere,
cathedrals hug the brute fact of themselves.
Earthquakes can tumble them, but too late; too late.
We walked for four days. There it was: a temple?
A solarium? Everything pointed at the sun.
The élan: how staircases seem to pour themselves;
how lintels form the cresting of an arch.
Bright water sparking everywhere the proof,
somehow, that something like bright spirits live
within it still; that something dances in
the air the conical hills all arch to meet
despite the bootprint of the Spanish stone.

# Music Club

We lay our iPhones down like winning hands.
Bagpipes and jazz and a voice so flat
it's like our own. A tramp's voice hangs in rags.
Each song's a burst of light: it simplifies
what it illuminates. Refracted in the choices
that we make, we all seem bolder, more alive,
and if I do the things I sometimes do —
if I perform the things I feel or indiscriminately
blare, like a kazoo — then what we can agree
upon is this: that truth resides wherever the music is.

## Music Club (Remix)

I'm a cartoon:
an ersatz rage
balloons and then deflates
like fire in a hearth;
the distaff side
of hurling songs,
like plates,
into the air.
We place our phones
like winning hands
but who can really understand
why someone loves a song?
A voice scrappy as rags;
an organ, prowling like a cat;
slack drums.
The anger is enthusiasm, squared.
Another means of entertainment;
difficult fun.

# Iceland

Trump in the White House and I think about
the frailty of things: the carpark, dark,
still, in the middle of the day, its lights
weirdly intent; the pond which was the opposite
of a miracle: the mystery of water become solid.
Out past the streets, the air insists
on its own power; on how the world
can be shredded sideways, become a great and furious
giddiness. Under the glacier, one chapel echoed
while the other seemed to gather every word.
Anti-sonorous, austerely serious,
it was determined to refute the world
outside; you, yes, but more: all of its signs
— the feral, furious snow and warring winds.

## New Year's Eve

*Top of the Pops*;
all alien now.
How you judge pleasure
on your skin,
and how its syntax
seems to have moved beyond you.

A *round* sound:
ping-pong, but more so,
coloured, synthetic balls
(it sounds like)
struck just like a glockenspiel.
That G-force chorus.
Ragga. Then "Havana"
like a well-worn dress;
somebody else's slinkiness
approximated and subdued.

Later, Jools Holland,
which was worse.
Jose Feliciano,
arms and neck and torso
fused together,

mimicking himself;
his voice and fingers clever
as they used to be
but in exactly the same way.
Most of the singers are so old
that age is like sand
gathered in their throat.
The band gives every note its due;
no more nor less.
At least the playlist that my friend made
lifts and boils:
grammar as clear as water
and, yes, ineffable.

# Osteopath

It counts as speech
to roll my neck
and bend towards the floor.
Held down,
my flesh begins to rise;
finds its knowledge of itself renewed.
Sometimes she'll close her eyes
and use two fingers, like a dial.
Something — a lapse
into gratitude or resignation —
spreads. It's like a smile. Later,
my body fights itself again.
It nags and burns.
It has learned nothing;
can only contract,
being its own experience.

## Dancers

It looked exactly like itself:
plaster like flaking pastry;
alleys, steeped in darkness,
where light dithered on the canals.
The water rolled gently in
place, like sleep. When our boat
made the slow arc to St Mark's,
the sea and sky appeared to be
one thing. It felt like flying.

Elsewhere, the water smelted light
until it looked like heat.
The whole town's quietly proclaiming sex:
the boats' prows and the concupiscence
of the waves, water and light co-mingling,
the houses all pretending privacy
with such rococo gestures
that you know they're signalling its opposite.
Reflections seemed to muss the water's hair;
to ease themselves on top of it.

It was Carnival. In our hotel,
masked dancers formed a frieze,

moved by a breath
of wind. They danced
in that eerie clockwork
that you see in dreams.
Pretending to be permanently arched,
like upraised statues,
on their feet
they mimed a state of grace
that's really death,
as all would-be perfection is.

Outside, people were dressed as
Tetris shapes. In Harry's Bar, you
weren't allowed to move the chairs.
The gondoliers resented you.
But, in the restaurant, the
dancers all displayed
a giddy furtiveness. They
lurked around the toilets in white
wigs and tinselly brocade. Like the
canals, the gap between experience and
expectation was dissolved in the bright,
fluid world of appearances.

# Reverse Haiku

Arc lamps on the cabbage patch
and a blot of fur
as still as gathered moonlight.

## Tuscany

When the storm came, it knocked the power out.
One candle juggled with the dark while rain
annulled the world outside. In the morning, the sun
seemed cruel: it had already burnt the sunflowers
down to matchsticks; had bullied the land so that
it lay supine beneath it. But the sky was itself again:
each cloud defined its depth; made it seem louder.
In San Gimignano, the towers had been transformed
into stone waterfalls: something you drive
to see, not subject to time's rules. But look
at how the paintings glower with gold. Bright gloss,
honeying everything. What is it meant to be?
God, shining like a flower? A prince's imprimatur?
Or the sun: the way it burns everything to dross.

# It Will All Be Discarded in the End

It will all be discarded in the end:
the sea and strand; the ordinary light.
Days topple into days 'til night descends.

Useless to try to make the world your friend;
to make your peace with the approaching blight.
It will all be discarded in the end.

Rivers abide; they seem sometimes to tend
our withering crop of booty, pale and slight.
Days topple into days 'til night descends.

You end up being an uneasy blend
of you and it: the world and its delights.
It will all be discarded in the end.

You make a pact. You try not to offend
the forces dark, the terrible forces bright.
Days topple into days as night descends.

You're not given a thing, though world has blent
itself with you. You're just an acolyte.
It will all be discarded in the end.
Days topple into days then night descends.

# Acknowledgements

The gears of the poetry world grind exceptionally slowly. (There are magazines — I will do them the favour of not naming them — that don't let you know what's happened to your submission for at least a year.) In other words, I was lucky enough to receive an offer of publication before most of these poems had found a home. Nevertheless, some of my poems have appeared in *Alba*, *The High Window*, *Obsessed With Pipework*, *Ink Sweat and Tears*, *The Interpreter's House*, *One Hand Clapping* and *Acumen*. They have also been featured on the *Social But Distanced* podcast and at the Islamabad Literary Festival. My thanks to all of them.

Thanks too to my publisher, Vine Leaves Press, and to Melanie Faith, my excellent (and very encouraging) editor. Thanks and my love to Naomi, as always, and thanks to Chas, Peter and Richard, without whom the Music Club poems — and an awful lot of fantastic evenings — would not have existed. Finally, a big hug and all my love to my daughter Alice, who inspired my favourite poem in the collection and who I hope will one day work her way through this book and all the rest of them.

"After Larkin" is based on "Deceptions" by Philip Larkin. "Thirteen Ways of Looking at David Bowie" is hopefully an obvious allusion to Wallace Stevens, while "Insomniacs" in the same sequence is an adaptation of "Another Lullaby for Insomniacs" by A. E. Stallings. I'm grateful to all for the inspiration.